TIME FOR KIDS READERS

The Exile of Roger Williams

by Randi Hacker

Harcourt

Orlando   Austin   Chicago   New York   Toronto   London   San Diego

Visit *The Learning Site!*
www.harcourtschool.com

A Little About

In London, England, at the start of the 1600s, a son was born to a tailor named James Williams and his wife, Alice. The baby, one of four children, was christened Roger in St. Sepulchre's Church. Like many other London buildings, it was destroyed in the Great Fire of 1666. The records of Roger's birth were lost, so his actual birth date is unknown. But that doesn't really matter. For Roger Williams grew up to make his mark far from

Young Roger

London. His legacy in New England, in North America, has lasted hundreds of years.

Young Roger became a chaplain of the Church of England in 1629. Soon after, he fell in love with a young woman. When her family refused to let them marry, Roger became ill. He was nursed back to health by Mary Barnard, who lived nearby. They were married on December 15, 1629.

Facing the Unknown

In 1630, Roger and Mary Williams boarded a small ship in England. They were about to sail across the ocean to a place in North America called Massachusetts. They knew that many hardships awaited them. Many of the people who had gone on the journey before them had drowned in storms at sea or died from disease, starvation, or cold weather in North America. Still the married couple got on the ship.

Why were Roger and Mary Williams willing to risk the dangers of the journey? Why were they willing to face the hardships of life in a different land? To them, the reason was simple. They hoped to find religious freedom. They wanted to find a place where they could practice their religion the way they chose.

The Massachusetts Colony had been settled in 1620 by Puritans, people from England also known as Pilgrims. The Puritans were Protestants, like most English people at that time. However, Puritans strongly disagreed with the practices of the Church of England. So the Puritans fled. When they landed in North America, they built a colony.

Roger and Mary Williams were also Puritans. In fact, Roger Williams had become a well-known Puritan minister. When he landed in Massachusetts, Governor John Winthrop greeted him with open arms.

Winthrop soon changed his mind. Williams disagreed with the Puritan leaders on several important matters. Williams accused the Massachusetts Puritans of doing just what the church in England had done. The Pilgrims had strict laws to force the colonists to worship in the Puritan way. The Puritans had come to North America searching for religious freedom. Yet they were unwilling to give that same freedom to people with other beliefs.

Pilgrims built their houses in Massachusetts.

Williams spoke out against the church leaders. He tried to rally other colonists to his side, but he didn't find many followers. Williams not only believed in freedom of religion, he also said that the colonists did not have the right to take land from the American Indians. This idea was very unpopular. Like most European colonies, the Massachusetts colony was created on land taken from the Indians.

By speaking out, Williams got into a lot of trouble. He was brought to trial. The court found him guilty and sentenced him to be sent back to England. In the winter of 1636, he left his family and fled from the colony, barely avoiding capture.

The Friendly Wampanoag

The winter of 1636 in New England was stormy. The snow was deep. The cold was bitter. Williams might have died a few days after fleeing the colony if he hadn't come to a village. It was a village of the Wampanoag tribe in the area that is now Rhode Island. Chief Massasoit gave Williams a safe place to stay.

Williams spent that winter living with the Wampanoag and learning from them. He genuinely liked the Indians and was interested in their ways of life.

Unlike some other settlers, Williams respected the Indians and their beliefs. He did not think they had to have the same religion as he did. Williams's ideas about the Indians were rooted in his religious beliefs. He believed deeply in Christianity, but he never tried to get the Indians to believe as he did. He respected their right to believe as they wished.

Roger Williams's church in Salem, in the Massachusetts Bay Colony, wasn't fancy.

The pilgrims greet Massasoit, the leader of the Wampanoag Indians, with open arms.

A Place Called Providence

Roger Williams was welcomed by the Narragansett people to the land later called Rhode Island.

In 1636, after his winter with the Wampanoag, Roger Williams made his way to the Narragansett River. There he was given a piece of land by Canonicus, a *sachem,* or leader, of the Narragansett people. The Narragansetts' attitude toward the English changed when they met Roger Williams. Here was a man who believed that the English king had no right to Indian lands and was not afraid to say so. They admired Williams. They trusted him. That is why they deeded him the land that was to become Rhode Island.

On that land, by the Seekonk River, Williams founded the settlement of Providence. Today Providence is the capital of Rhode Island. The name means "gift of God." In the deed he received from the Narragansetts, Williams wrote down his beliefs about freedom of religion.

Now that he had a place to settle, Williams's wife and two daughters, Mary and Freeborn, joined him. Others came, too. Together they built the settlement of Providence. All those who settled there agreed that people would be allowed to worship as they chose. Over the next several years, more people settled in Providence. Three more towns were built: Portsmouth, Newport, and Warwick.

By 1643, the towns had grown so much that the people there wanted to remain independent from Massachusetts by becoming an official colony. Once more Roger Williams crossed the Atlantic Ocean. He went to ask King Charles I of England for a charter, official permission to form a colony. However, the first charter was granted by Parliament. The four towns became the colony that would form the core of Rhode Island.

King Charles I of England

Freedom for All

Rhode Island grew into a place where people of all religions were allowed to live in peace. That didn't mean Roger Williams agreed with them all. He spent his life strongly defending the principles he believed in. He disagreed with the Quakers, for example. When he was 69 years old, he rowed a boat from Providence to Newport, a distance of 30 miles (48 km), to hold a debate with the Quakers about their beliefs. However, even if Williams didn't agree with the Quaker religion, the Quakers were still free to worship as they wanted in Rhode Island.

Rhode Islanders proudly call their state "the first democracy." After being forced to flee other places because of their religion, many Jewish settlers found a home in Rhode Island. The seaside city of Newport has the oldest synagogue in the United States. The first Quaker meeting house was built in Newport, too. America's first Baptist church was formed in Providence. In their native land, the French Huguenots (HYOO•guh•nahts), were badly treated because of their religious beliefs. They found freedom in East Greenwich.

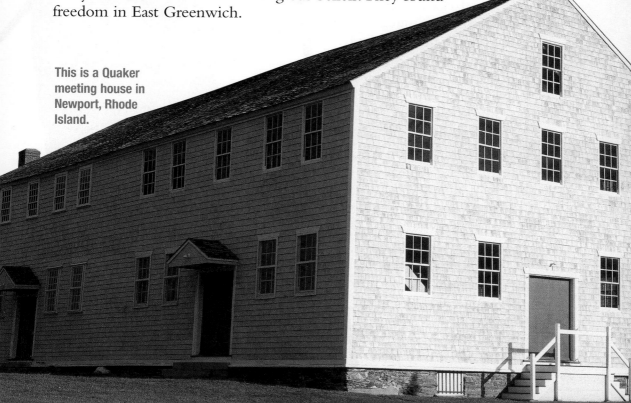

This is a Quaker meeting house in Newport, Rhode Island.

The colonists' relations with the local Indian tribes didn't turn out quite so well. The settlers and the Narragansetts respected Roger Williams for years of keeping the peace between them, but even he could not prevent the friendship from falling apart after a series of clashes. The result was one of the most terrible events in Rhode Island history.

It was a conflict called *King Philip's War.* King Philip was another name for Metacomet, the great Wanpanoag chief. From 1675 to 1676, several tribes fought to rid New England of all Europeans. Thousands of people died. Much property was destroyed. The Narragansetts did not, at first, take sides. However, they sought revenge after a sneak attack on their main village by a force from the Plymouth Colony in Massachusetts.

The Narragansetts attacked Providence and burned down most of the town. Roger Williams, who had survived and thrived there with the tribe's help, watched in horror. All his work seemed to go up in smoke. He was devastated.

The oldest synagogue in the United States is in Newport, Rhode Island.

The First Baptist Meetinghouse is in Providence, Rhode Island.

The Wampanoag and the Narragansett

Wampanoag means "people of the dawn." The tribe had that name because it lived in the east. The tribe lived by fishing, farming, hunting, and gathering. Wampanoag houses were made of woven mats stretched over wooden structures. When the tribe moved to the seacoast in the spring and summer, its members took their mats along, leaving the wooden structures behind for their return.

The real name of the Narragansett people is *Nanhigganeuck*. That means "people of the small point" in their language. Early sailors couldn't say it correctly and came up with Narragansett. The Dutch called them Nahican. Narragansett life was similar to the Wampanoag, but the two tribes were fierce enemies.

A statue of Roger Williams overlooks Providence.

The war ended with the killing of King Philip in 1676. The number of Indian tribes had been reduced greatly due to casualties, disease, and hunger. They united to form one tribe, taking the name Narragansett. These Native Americans still live in Rhode Island today.

Roger Williams may have been disappointed, but he never stopped working for Providence. He was the town clerk for many years. The exact date of his death is unknown. It was between January and March of 1683. He was buried in the orchard behind the land on which he'd first settled so many years before.

In 1936, Williams was reburied and his remains were placed under a statue honoring him. The statue of him looks out over the city he founded.

Williams was said to have died with little money or material possessions. He'd spent his life building Rhode Island instead of trying to become wealthy.

Religious freedom is granted in the First Amendment to the Constitution of the United States. It says:

"Congress shall make no law respecting an establishment of religion, or prohibiting the free exercise thereof."

We have Roger Williams to thank for that. He may have died without material riches, but he left another kind of wealth, one of ideas. He gave to this country the foundation for freedom and tolerance.

TFK SPOTLIGHT

ANNE HUTCHINSON

Roger Williams wasn't the only rebel forced to flee the Massachusetts colony. Anne Hutchinson was another colonist who stood up for her beliefs.

When Anne Hutchinson moved to Boston with her husband in 1634, she stood out. Not only did she disagree with the Puritan leaders, but she began preaching her own beliefs in her home. Hutchinson believed that simply following the religious law of the colony wasn't enough. Soon she attracted many followers, both men and women.

The Puritan leaders could not stand this challenge to their rule. Not only was she preaching against their beliefs, she was a woman! At that time women were not expected to express their ideas. They said she was no longer a member of their church and banished her from the colony.

The Hutchinson family went first to Portsmouth, Rhode Island. Later they moved to Newport, Rhode Island. After the death of her husband, William, Anne and her six youngest children moved to the Dutch colony of New Netherlands (present-day New York).

At that time, 1642, wars between the Native Americans and settlers were raging. Hutchinson and five of her children were killed by a Mahican war party in 1643. Her youngest daughter, Susanna, was captured by the Indians and lived with them.

Anne Hutchinson is considered one of the great women of history. She stood up for her beliefs despite the danger to her safety. She is one of the people we must thank for the religious freedom we enjoy in the United States today.